The Prestige S [Venture Transport]

Venture Transport

of Consett

G E Hutchinson F.C.I.T., F.I.L.T.

Cover: The heart of Venture was the Derwent Valley route number 11 between Consett, Shotley Bridge, Hamsterley, Rowlands Gill and Newcastle. This 1970 picture shows new Alexander-bodied Leyland Leopard No. **286** *(**HUP386H**) at Rowlands Gill en route for Newcastle shortly before the company was sold. (GEH)*

Inside front cover: The route map in the July 1965 timetable book showed the network very much at its most extensive before rural service withdrawals in the late 1960s. (GEH Collection)

Rear cover: The cover of the last timetable book issued by Venture in September 1969. The illustration shows the horse drawn "Venture" coach behind the modern bus. (GEH Collection)

Inside rear cover: An Albion Motors drawing showing the body details for an Albion PJ26 bus supplied to Reed Bros in 1929 (fleet No. **15**) *and appropriately lettered for the Venture route. (GEH Collection)*

Title page: The rural route from Consett to the attractive village of Blanchland in the North Pennines was popular with tourists in the summer months. 1958 Albion Aberdonian No. **200** *(**164BUP**) sets down passengers at Blanchland in summer 1966, some of whom may have transferred at Shotley Bridge off route 11 from Newcastle, which was a connection shown in the timetable. (GEH Collection)*

Opposite page: Between 1946 and 1948 Venture bought 60 Willowbrook-bodied Daimler CVD6 buses which became familiar on all routes until the mid 1950s. Fleet number **140** *was photographed at Consett between trips on route 11 in 1955. (GEH)*

Below: Fleet No. **140** *heads a line up of ten new Daimlers in 1947, photographed near Whittonstall. (GEH Collection)*

About the Author

Eric Hutchinson enjoyed a 33 year career in public transport in his native north-east of England. He joined Venture Transport at Consett in 1962 as a management trainee and later became Assistant to the General Manager. In 1970, when Venture was sold, he left to join the new Tyneside Passenger Transport Executive. By 1975 he was the PTE's Director of Integrated Operations and was very much involved in the integration of bus services with the Tyne and Wear Metro. In 1986 he was appointed Chairman and Managing Director of Busways Travel Services Limited, which had been formed to take over the former PTE bus operations in Newcastle, South Shields and Sunderland. In 1989 he led the management and employee buyout of Busways from the Tyne and Wear Passenger Transport Authority. He subsequently negotiated the sale of this successful 600-vehicle company to Stagecoach Holdings in 1994.

Introduction

The Venture Transport Company (Newcastle) Limited was formed in 1938 by the owners of Reed Brothers Limited and Venture Bus Services Limited to amalgamate their businesses after a period of development going back to 1912. Both had been pioneer bus operators in the Derwent Valley area of County Durham. Of course recollections of Venture Transport as it was in the 1960s are still relatively clear, but as time goes by features of the earlier years are remembered much less. This publication is not a detailed history, but is intended to portray the flavour of a successful privately owned business that provided essential passenger transport services in an area also served by two of the strongest territorial companies: The Northern General Transport Co Ltd and United Automobile Services Ltd.

The Derwent Valley and its adjacent areas contained many coal mining settlements and there was the Consett Iron Company's steel-making plant at Consett, a town almost 900 feet above sea level. The local bus routes developed to link these communities and there were frequent main road routes to Newcastle upon Tyne. So successful were these that the rail service in the Derwent Valley was in decline from the 1920s and was finally closed to passengers on 1st February 1954.

The round the clock nature of steel making and coal mining produced opportunities for efficient operation of buses, as the peak travel times for these industries did not conflict with travel to work and scholars travel peaks; thus Venture buses worked long days and high mileages, but they were always single-deckers because of the number of low bridges in the areas served.

The territory covered ranged from the City of Newcastle, through the lower stretches of the Tyne and Derwent valleys, to the steep climb into Consett and wild moorland areas to its west. Although most of the routes were in well-populated localities, there were rural routes to the west, serving places such as Stanhope and Blanchland in the North Pennines and also Whittonstall, Hexham, and Hedley on the Hill. Harsh winter weather tested the endurance of crews and buses, but there was a determination to "get through" even in extreme conditions.

The Early Years

Reed Brothers Ltd originated from a garage business at Sunniside, in which all five brothers had an interest. An Iris charabanc was acquired in 1912 and they used it on a route from Bensham tram terminus to the villages of Whickham, Sunniside, Marley Hill and Burnopfield. A new Halley charabanc was obtained in 1914, but the business lapsed during the 1914-18 War when the Halley chassis was commandeered by the Government. However, in early 1918 two Albion buses were purchased for use on a route between Chopwell, Hamsterley Colliery, Rowlands Gill and Newcastle, which commenced in September 1918. In 1919 the business became a limited company.

Venture Bus Services Ltd had its origins in a motor bus route started shortly after the 1914-18 War by Messrs Harper and Lockey. This ran through the Derwent Valley between Shotley Bridge, Hamsterley Colliery, Rowlands Gill and Newcastle. The business was acquired by Mr G R Harrison and Mr W T Richardson, who decided to use the fleetname "Venture". A well-known sight in the Derwent Valley was the horse drawn four-in-hand Venture coach owned by Major Priestman, a local colliery proprietor. He gave his permission for the name to be used for the bus service.

In 1925 Reed Brothers joined with Harrison and Richardson in the operation of the Venture bus route between Newcastle and Shotley Bridge which was then extended to the steel town of Consett. In 1929 Harrison and Richardson formed their business into a limited company: Venture Bus Services Ltd. They garaged their red and white-liveried vehicles at Low Westwood. Also in 1929, Reed Brothers moved their green-liveried fleet from Sunniside to premises at Park Road, Blackhill near Consett.

Expansion in the 1930s

No doubt in anticipation of the regulatory proposals in the Road Traffic Act 1930, in that year Reed Brothers and Venture Bus Services made an agreement to operate their bus routes jointly and to pool receipts. This arrangement operated under the trading name "Venture & Reed Bros" They opened a joint office in Front Street, Consett and adopted a yellow and maroon fleet livery. The two companies continued to own their separate assets but by 1934 similar vehicle types were being bought for both fleets. Interestingly, even fleet numbers were given to Venture vehicles and odd to Reed vehicles.

Acquisitions then became the key feature. On 26th April 1930 Reed Bros took over that part of the business of J E Walker of Edmundbyers known as the "Pioneer Bus Service" which ran between Blanchland, Edmundbyers, Shotley Bridge and Consett. They then turned their sights on the two Chopwell based bus operators (J R & R B Parker and J Clydesdale) who jointly provided important routes between Chopwell, Hamsterley Colliery or High Spen, Rowlands Gill and Newcastle. Reed Bros acquired Parker and Clydesdale went to Venture, both in August 1930.

Expansion and consolidation was now well underway and the next target was the partnership of Robson Brothers, who operated from bases at Consett and High Spen with a fleet of about 25 buses

SHOTLEY BRIDGE AND NEWCASTLE.

Week-days Dep.	a.m.	p.m.	p.m.	p.m.	p.m.	W. & S. p.m.	p.m.	Sundays a.m.	p.m.	p.m.	p.m.	p.m.
SHOTLEY BRIDGE	9.20	12.40	3.40	6.40	8.50	8.50	11.10	9.0	1.30	3.40	8.50	10.50
EBCHESTER ..	9.25	12.45	3.45	6.45	8.55	8.55	11.15	9.5	1.35	3.45	8.55	10.55
HAMSTERLEY ..	9.30	12.50	3.50	6.50	9.0	9.0	11.20	9.10	1.40	3.50	9.0	11.0
LINTZ FORD ..	9.35	12.55	3.55	6.55		9.5		9.15	1.45	3.55	9.5	
ROWLANDS GILL	9.40	1.0	4.0	7.0		9.10		9.20	1.50	4.0	9.10	
WINLATON MILL	9.50	1.10	4.10	7.10		9.20		9.30	2.0	4.10	9.20	
SWALWELL BRIDGE	9.55	1.15	4.15	7.15		9.25		9.35	2.5	4.15	9.25	
SCOTSWOOD BGE.	10.0	1.20	4.20	7.20		9.30		9.40	2.10	4.20	9.30	
NEWCASTLE arr	10.10	1.30	4.30	7.30		9.40		9.50	2.20	4.30	9.40	

Leaving Clayton Garage, (round corner from Jackson's of Clayton Street.)

Weekdays	a.m.	p.m.	p.m.	p.m.	W. & S. p m	Sundays a.m.	p.m.	p.m.	p.m.
NEWCASTLE dep	10.50	1.50	4.50	7.50	10.20	10.0	2.30	7.30	10.0
SCOTSWOOD BGE.	11.0	2.0	5.0	8.0	10.30	10.10	2.40	7.40	10.10
SWALWELL BRIDGE	11.5	2.5	5.5	8.5	10.35	10.15	2.45	7.45	10.15
WINLATON MILL	11.10	2.10	5.10	8.10	10.40	10.20	2.50	7.50	10.20
ROWLANDS GILL	11.20	2.20	5.20	8.20	10.50	10.30	3.0	8.0	10.30
LINTZ FORD ..	11.25	2.25	5.25	8.25	10.55	10.35	3.5	8.5	10.35
HAMSTERLEY ..	11.30	2.30	5.30	8.30	11.0	10.40	3.10	8.10	10.40
EBCHESTER ..	11.35	2.35	5.35	8.35	11.5	10.45	3.15	8.15	10.45
SHOTLEY BGE. arr	11.40	2.40	5.40	8.40	11.10	10.50	3.20	8.20	10.50

W. & S. DENOTES WEDNESDAYS AND SATURDAYS.

TEAM VALLEY PRINTING WORKS, BIRTLEY.

Above: The timetable for Harper and Lockey's bus service introduced after the 1914-18 war. Below: The cover of the Venture and Reed Bros timetable folder for all routes issued in 1934. (Both: GEH Collection)

painted in a yellow and black livery. Venture & Reed Bros formed a new joint company, Robson Brothers Ltd, for this acquisition and in 1933 transferred the Consett branch of the business.

The key part of this was a route between Consett, Medomsley, Rowlands Gill and Newcastle. There was also a local service in the Consett area running to Leadgate and the Hat & Feather Inn. Next, in 1934, the remainder of the Robson business was transferred. This part, known as the "Yellow Bus Service" and based at High Spen, operated an important route between Chopwell, High Spen, Greenside, Ryton and Newcastle. There were also routes between Greenside and Newcastle via Folly and between Crawcrook, Greenside and Hedley on the Hill. The yellow and black livery was retained for the Robson operations.

Then, on 4th December 1934, Robson Bros Ltd was used to purchase the business of Mrs Annie Bessford of Swinbourne House, High Spen, who operated hourly on the important route between High Spen, Highfield, Rowlands Gill and Newcastle.

There was no doubt a need to tidy up the structures of the companies after these acquisitions. On 10th March 1938 all of the businesses were incorporated into a new limited company, The Venture Transport Company (Newcastle) Limited, with its registered office at 16/17, Princes Street, Consett. There were depots at Blackhill, Low Westwood and High Spen. The total bus fleet numbered 62: 19 from Reed Bros, 19 from Venture and 24 ex-Robson Bros vehicles. The yellow and maroon livery previously used by Venture and Reed Bros was to be applied to all buses.

VENTURE & REED BROS

PHONE:- CONSETT 282

The Venture Bus Service Ltd. Hamsterley Colliery

Reed Bros. Ltd. Blackhill 'Phone CONSETT 282

OFFICIAL TIME TABLE FOLDER
GRATIS

SHOWING JOINT SERVICES OPERATED BY
REED BROS. LTD., BLACKHILL,
AND THE
VENTURE BUS SERVICE LTD.,
HAMSTERLEY COLLIERY,

SHOWING ALSO SERVICES OPERATED BY
ROBSON BROS., LTD.

WITH THE COMPLIMENTS OF VENTURE &
REED BROS., LTD.,
BLACKHILL

BESSFORD'S BUS SERVICE, HIGH SPEN TO NEWCASTLE.

(Highfield, Rowlands Gill, Swalwell Bridge and Scotswood).

Proprietor: A. BESSFORD, Swinbourne House, High Spen. 'Phone: Chopwell 5.

	MONDAYS TO SATURDAYS.					Wed. & Sat.only	Saturday only			SUNDAYS.				
	a.m. dep.	a.m. depart	a.m. depart		p.m. depart	p.m. depart	p.m. depart	a.m. depart	p.m. dep.		p.m. depart	p.m. depart	p.m. depart	p.m. depart
High Spen	7.13	8.13	9.13	then every hour until	9.13	10.13	10.13	10.13	1.13	then every hour until	8.13	9.13	9.43	10.13
Highfield	7.17	8.17	9.17		9.17	10.17	10.17	10.17	1.17		8.17	9.17	9.47	10.17
Rowlands Gill	7.22	8.22	9.22		9.22	10.22	10.22	10.22	1.22		8.22	9.22	9.52	10.22
Winlaton Mill	7.29	8.29	9.29		9.29	10.29	10.29	10.29	1.29		8.29	9.29	9.59	10.29
Swalwell Bridge	7.33	8.33	9.33		9.33	10.33	10.33	10.33	1.33		8.33	9.33	10.3	10.33
Newcastle (arrive)	7.50	8.50	9.50		9.50	10.50	10.50	10.50	1.50		8.50	9.50	10.20	10.50

	depart	depart	depart		depart	depart	depart	depart	depart		depart	depart	depart	depart
Newcastle	8.25	9.25	10.25	then every hour until	10.25	10.55	11.25	11.25	2.25	then every hour until	9.25	9.55	10.25	11.25
Swalwell Bridge	8.42	9.42	10.42		10.42	11.12	11.42	11.42	2.42		9.42	10.12	10.42	11.42
Winlaton Mill	8.46	9.46	10.46		10.46	11.16	11.46	11.46	2.46		9.46	10.16	10.46	11.46
Rowlands Gill	8.53	9.53	10.53		10.53	11.23	11.53	11.53	2.53		9.53	10.23	10.53	11.53
Highfield	8.58	9.58	10.58		10.58	11.28	11.58	11.58	2.58		9.58	10.28	10.58	11.58
High Spen (arrive)	9.03	10.03	11.03		11.03	11.33	12.03	12.03	3.03		10.03	10.33	11.03	12.03

Mrs Annie Bessford's 1933 timetable. (GEH Collection)

The routes being operated at this time are listed below:-

2 Consett, Whittonstall, Riding Mill, Hexham
3 Consett, Shotley Bridge, Edmundbyers, Blanchland, Townfield
5 Consett, Medomsley, High Westwood, Rowlands Gill, Newcastle
7 Consett, Leadgate, Hat & Feather Inn
11 Consett, Shotley Bridge, Hamsterley Colliery, Rowlands Gill, Newcastle (*a)
14 Shotley Bridge, Edmundbyers, Stanhope
15 Chopwell, Hedley on the Hill
22 Chopwell, High Spen, Greenside, Ryton, Blaydon, Newcastle
30 Consett, Shotley Bridge, Hamsterley Colliery, Chopwell (*b)
33 Chopwell, High Spen, Highfield, Rowlands Gill, Newcastle
44 High Spen, Greenside, Folly, Blaydon, Newcastle
55 Crawcrook, Greenside, Hedley on the Hill
(N.B. Route numbers are shown for reference as these came in soon afterwards. * Joint with Northern General Transport: a=75% Venture, 25% Northern; b=50% each.)

Soon afterwards, in 1938, three new local routes were operating in Consett:-
4 Consett, Blackhill, Bridgehill
6 Consett, Templetown
8 Consett, Crookhall

These were the last route developments before the 1939-45 war.

The 1939-45 War and into the 1950s

With the approach of the 1939-45 War the new Venture Transport had a reasonably modern fleet to see it through this troubled period; 35 new buses had been delivered between 1937 and 1939, as detailed later. Like all bus companies, Venture Transport faced heavy demands during the war and emerged with its older buses in urgent need of replacement. One new route was introduced in 1944, between Hedley on the Hill, Greenside and Newcastle (77), but others were curtailed in this period.

After the war a period of expansion followed and 60 new buses were delivered between 1946 and 1948. Demand for bus travel was growing and the company launched new routes and extended others:-

66 Winlaton Mill, Newcastle (new 1946)
22 High Spen, Victoria Garesfield local (new 1946)
9 Consett, Shotley Bridge Hospital, Elm Park (new 1947, joint with Northern General)
10 Consett, Oakdale Estate (new 1947, joint with Northern General)
12 Consett, Medomsley, High Westwood (new 1948)
15 Extended from Hedley on the Hill to Prudhoe Station (1948)
55 Extended Crawcrook to South Wylam (1948)
17 High Spen, Rowlands Gill, Winlaton, Blaydon (new 1950)

TRAVEL BY THE PIONEERS OF
VENTURE AND REED BROS
THE DERWENT VALLEY ROUTE

Joint Traffic Office : 60a Front Street, Consett

PHONE ... ... CONSETT 282

Consett : Newcastle

via Blackhill, Shotley Bridge, Hamsterley and Rowlands Gill.

MONDAYS to SATURDAYS.

	a.m	a.m	a.m	a.m	a.m	a.m	a.m	a.m	a.m	a.m		p m	p m	p m	p m	p m	p m	p m	p m	p m	p m
																			s		
Consett ...dep	5 15	5 35	5 50	6 25	6 55	7 15	7 25	7 40	7 55	8 40		9 40	9 55	1025	1025	1040	1055	1110	1140	1155	1210
Blackhill ...	5 20	5 40	5 55	6 30	7 0	7 20	7 30	7 45	8 0	8 45		9 45	10 0	1030	1030	1045	11 0	1115	1145	12 0	1215
Shotley Bridge ...	5 26	5 46	6 1	6 36	7 6	7 26	7 36	7 51	8 6	8 36	8 51	9 51	10 6	1036	1036	1051	11 6	1121	1151		1221
Ebchester, ...	5 32	5 52	6 7	6 42	7 12	7 32	7 42	7 57	8 12	8 42	8 57	9 57	1012	1042	1042	1057		1127			1227
Hamsterley ...	5 37	5 57	6 12	6 47	7 17	7 37	7 47	8 2	8 17	8 47	9 2	10 2	1017	1047	1047	11 2		1132			1232
Lintz Ford ...	5 42	6 2	6 17	6 52	7 22	7 43	7 52	8 7	8 22	8 52	9 8	10 8	1022	1052							
Rowlands Gill ...	5 47	6 7	6 22	6 57	7 27	7 49	7 57	8 12	8 27	8 57	9 14	1014	1027	1057							
Winlaton Mill ...	5 54	6 14	6 29	7 4	7 34	7 56	8 4	8 19	8 34	9 4	9 21	1021	1034	11 4							
Swalwell ...	5 58	6 18	6 33	7 8	7 38	8 0	8 8	8 23	8 38	9 8	9 25	1025	1038	11 8							
Scotswood ...	6 1	6 21	6 36	7 11	7 41	8 3	8 11	8 26	8 41	9 11	9 28	1028	1041	1111							
Newcastle arr	6 31	6 46	7 21	7 51	8 13	8 21	8 36	8 51	9 21	9 38		1038	1051	1121							

	a.m	a.m	a.m	a.m	a.m	a.m	a.m	a.m	a.m	a.m		p m	p m	p m	p m	p m	p m	p m	p m	p m	p m
														s							
Newcastle dep		6 45	6 55	7 40	8 0	8 25	8 35	8 50	9 5	9 35	9 50	1050	11 5	1150							
Scotswood ...	6 5	7 0	7 10	7 53	8 15	8 40	8 45	9 3	9 15	9 45	10 3	11 3	1115	12 3							
Swalwell ...	6 10	7 4	7 14	7 57	8 19	8 44	8 48	9 7	9 18	9 48	10 7	11 7	1118	12 7							
Winlaton Mill ...	6 13	7 8	7 18	8 1	8 23	8 48	8 52	9 11	9 22	9 52	1011	1111	1122	1211							
Rowlands Gill ..	6 20	7 15	7 25	8 8	8 30	8 55	8 59	9 18	9 29	9 59	1018	1118	1129	1218							
Lintz Ford ...	6 25	7 20	7 30	8 13	8 35	9 0	9 5	9 23	9 35	10 5	1023	1123	1135	1223							
Hamsterley ...	6 30	7 25	7 35	8 18	8 40	9 5	9 12	9 30	9 42	1012	1030	1130	1142	1230							
Ebchester ...	6 35	7 30	7 40	8 22	8 45	9 10	9 16	9 34	9 46	1016	1034	1134	1146	1234							
Shotley Bridge ...	6 40	7 35	7 45	8 28	8 50	9 15	9 22	9 40	9 52	1022	1040	1140	1152	1240							
Blackhill ...	6 47	7 42	7 52	8 35	8 57	9 22	9 30	9 48	10 0	1030	1048	1148	12 0	1248							
Consett arr	6 55	7 50	8 0	8 41	9 5	9 30	9 36	9 54	10 6	1036	1054	1154	12 6	1254							

S: Saturdays only.

SUNDAYS.

	a m	a m	a m	a m	a m	a m	a m	a m	a m	a m		p m	p m	p m	p m	p m	p m	p m	p m	p m	p m
Consett dep	5 15	6 45	7 45	8 55	9 25	9 55	1025	1055	1125	1140		9 40	9 55	1025	1040	1055	1110	1140	1155	1210
Blackhill ...	5 20	6 50	7 50	9 0	9 30	10 0	1030	11 0	1130	1145		9 45	10 0	1030	1045	11 0	1115	1145	12 0	1215
Shotley Bridge ...	5 26	6 56	7 56	9 6	9 36	10 6	1036	11 6	1136	1151		9 51	10 6	1036	1051	11 6	1121	1151		1221
Ebchester ...	5 32	7 2	8 2	9 12	9 42	1012	1042	1112	1142	1157		9 57	1012	1042	1057		1127			1227
Hamsterley ...	5 37	7 7	8 7	9 17	9 47	1017	1047	1117	1147	12 2		10 2	1017	1047	11 2		1132			1232
Lintz Ford ...	5 42	7 12	8 12	9 22	9 52	1022	1052	1122	1152	12 8		10 8	1022							
Rowlands Gill ...	5 47	7 17	8 17	9 27	9 57	1027	1057	1127	1157	1214		1014	1027							
Winlaton Mill ...	5 54	7 24	8 24	9 34	10 4	1034	11 4	1134	12 4	1221		1021	1034							
Swalwell ...	5 58	7 28	8 28	9 38	10 8	1038	11 8	1138	12 8	1225		1025	1038							
Scotswood ...	6 1	7 31	8 31	9 41	1011	1041	1111	1141	1211	1228		1028	1041							
Newcastle arr		7 41	8 41	9 51	1021	1051	1121	1151	1221	1238		1038	1051							

	a m	a m	a m	a m	a m	a m	a m	a m	a m	a m		p m	p m	p m	p m	p m	p m	p m	p m	p m	p m
Newcastle dep		8 5	8 55	10 5	1035	11 5	1135	12 5	1235	1250		1050	11 5							
Scotswood ...	6 5	8 9	8	1015	1045	1115	1145	1215	1245	1 3		11 3	1115							
Swalwell ...	6 10	8 22	9 12	1018	1048	1118	1148	1218	1248	1 7		11 7	1118							
Winlaton Mill ...	6 13	8 26	9 17	1022	1052	1122	1152	1222	1252	1 11		1118	1129							
Rowlands Gill ...	6 20	8 33	9 25	1029	1059	1129	1159	1229	1259	1 18		1123	1135							
Lintzford ...	6 25	8 38	9 30	1035	11 5	1135	12 5	1235	1 5	1 23		1130	1142							
Hamsterley ...	6 30	8 43	9 35	1042	1142	1212	1242	1 12	1 30			1134	1146							
Ebchester ...	6 35	8 47	9 39	1046	1116	1146	1216	1246	1 16	1 34		1140	1152							
Shotley Bridge ...	6 41	8 53	9 45	1052	1122	1152	1222	1252	1 0	1 30	1 48	1148	12 0							
Blackhill ...	6 48	9 0	9 52	11 0	1130	12 0	1230	1 0	1 0	1 30	1 48	1154	12 6							
Consett arr	6 55	9 6	10 0	11 6	1136	12 6	1236	1 6	1 36	1 54										

Buses leaving Chopwell 24 miutes past the hour connect at Hamsterley Bank Top for Consett

The 40 minutes past the hour from Consett connects at Hamsterley for Chopwell.

LOOK OUT FOR THE BUS WITH THE GREEN SPOT LIGHT

26/12/33.

Ramsden Williams, Printer, Ann Street, Consett (Phone 150.)

The timetable for the Venture and Reed Bros "Derwent Valley Route" in 1933. At this stage the buses had a green spotlight to distinguish them from their competitors. (GEH Collection)

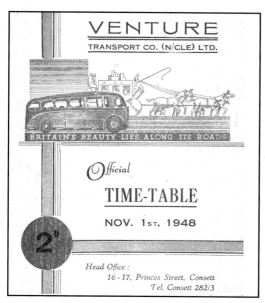

Above: The cover of Venture Transport's 1948 timetable book. Below: A 1963 Consett local newspaper advertisement. Taxis were a new feature and the mobile caravans for hire were converted from withdrawn 1947 and 1948 Daimler buses, initially for hire to employees; they were later hired to the general public. (Both: GEH Collection)

A further acquisition was made in 1951, in the Stanley area, which was a Northern General stronghold and which had not previously been served by Venture. The C & E Bus Co Ltd, owned by Messrs Colpitts and Ellwood, operated 13 buses on two routes between Stanley, Annfield Plain, Dipton and Flint Hill. These were given route numbers 25 and 31. Twelve buses transferred to Venture, but were at once withdrawn and replaced by Venture buses operating "on hire" to the C & E. This practice continued right to the end of Venture's existence as C & E was kept as a subsidiary company.

Service developments continued. In 1952 route 44 was diverted at Greenside to serve Rockwood Hill Estate rather than High Spen, then in 1953 route 17 was extended from Blaydon via Stella and across the Tyne to Newburn - an area then only served by Newcastle Corporation Transport. A new route 13 was introduced in 1953 linking Chopwell, Hamsterley Colliery, Shotley Bridge Hospital, Medomsley Edge and Leadgate. An important development in 1954 was the introduction of local routes in Prudhoe, to Drawback and Prudhoe Hall, as extensions of route 15, in an area then dominated by United Automobile Services.

The Mid Fifties and into the Sixties

By the mid 1950s the effects of private motoring and home television entertainment replacing cinemas began to be felt by Venture, as they were by most other bus companies. Venture Transport was still generally restricted to single-deck buses for passage beneath low bridges and duplicates were widely provided at peak times. The availability of larger buses enabled good economies to be made. The first underfloor engined vehicles were bought in 1955 and thereafter new buses were bought every year up to 1970, when the company was sold.

Driver-only operation was launched in 1959, initially on the rural services. This was successful and was continually extended, both for reasons of economy and to maintain full reliability when staff recruitment was not always easy. A rapid run down of the area's coal mines occurred in this period, which resulted in the decline and withdrawal of special services provided for miners. Generally the steel works at Consett continued to do well, although there were periods of recession. This was thus a period of change and Venture's management was keen to innovate and look for new opportunities as the traditional industries, which had provided good business, went further into decline. It was clear that the rural services were also in decline. It was decided to ensure that the best standards were achieved on the key routes to Newcastle and on the Consett local routes, with frequency enhancements where possible.

The introduction of 36ft-long buses from 1963, with more attractive interiors and seating, led to greater comfort for passengers and further operational efficiencies. Regular intakes of new coaches enhanced the private hire and tour business. There was diversification into running taxis, a car garage business and a public house near the Derwent reservoir.

Service developments were a continuing feature and in March 1961 route 55 was extended across the Tyne from South Wylam to North Wylam. In June 1961 additional trips were added to route 6 to serve the new Consett Iron Company steel plant at Hounsgill - an interesting example of a public bus service running into a private industrial site. The next advance was made in Prudhoe in October 1961 with the introduction of a further extension of route 15 to produce a local route between Prudhoe Station, Prudhoe main street and the new West Wylam Estate. In January 1964, because of decline, the local trips on route 22 between High Spen and Victoria Garesfield were withdrawn, but in May 1964 route 13 was extended from Leadgate to Consett.

At this time it was decided to look for further developments in new areas, as had been happening in Prudhoe. The western suburbs of Newcastle seemed a possibility and on 30th May 1964 route 17 was extended from Newburn to Lemington. This covered a section of road served by one of Newcastle Corporation's trunk routes. The outcome was encouraging. Venture gained from additonal passengers using its service to cross the Tyne via Newburn bridge as well as a share of the passengers between Newburn and Lemington. A further development into Newcastle Corporation territory took place in November 1965 with the extension of route 17 northwards via Union Hall Road and Lemington Road End to the new Chapel House Estate.

Newcastle Corporation resisted these changes before the Traffic Commissioners but Venture achieved its objectives, particularly as these extensions produced new transport links which were judged to be in the public interest. Chapel House Estate was further developed and Venture route 17, together with those of Newcastle Corporation and United, covered the full estate from August 1967.

In October 1965 rural route 3 was diverted between Blanchland and Townfield via Ramshaw to replace a withdrawal by Rochester & Marshall. Connections were set up in Blanchland with the R & M bus for Hexham. A further development occurred in Prudhoe in March 1966 when route 15 was diverted to serve more of West Wylam Estate and frequencies were enhanced on this route. January 1967 saw route 12 (Consett, High Westwood) withdrawn, mainly as a consequence of

the demolition of the former mining village of Allendale Cottages; replacement facilities were provided by a diversion of route 13 via Medomsley and changes to part of route 5 in this area which was renumbered 5/12.

Rural service changes were also continuing apace. In March 1967 route 2 was withdrawn from the Saturdays-only section between Whittonstall, Riding Mill and Hexham. This was followed in April 1967 by the elimination of route 77 between Greenside and Hedley on the Hill, although in February 1968 school-time journeys were introduced on service 55 for the section between Greenside and Coalburns. An optimistic move however, was the July 1967 diversion of routes 3 and 14 at Carterway Heads, to serve the company's public house, The Bolbec Manor House Inn. At the time this was said to be a response to the recently introduced breathalyser, so that patrons could get safely to the pub for their drink.

1968 to 1970 - Quality Service: More Rural Withdrawals

A significant development in 1968 was the introduction of a coordinated pattern of routes from Newcastle along the south side of the Tyne in conjunction with United. This directly involved Venture routes 15, 22, 44 and 55 and there were consequential changes to routes 17 and 33; in fact the whole of High Spen depot's operation was rescheduled. United routes involved were those from Newcastle to Ryton Village, High Spen, Stargate, Clara Vale, Scales Cross, Branch End and Hexham. The outcome was the creation of an even five-minute frequency on the main road via Blaydon and Ryton, with eight buses per hour provided by United and four by Venture. United withdrew their Newcastle, Greenside, High Spen route and Venture route 44 was split into two, with one part becoming new route 24 serving new areas of Greenside and Folly as well as Ryton.

Venture left the local services in Prudhoe to United. These had shown good potential, but were hampered by the hopelessly uneconomic route between Chopwell and Prudhoe, necessary as a positioning run for buses to reach Prudhoe; this rural route was abandoned when the coordination scheme was introduced on 28 April 1968.

In September 1968 there were further rural service cuts: route 2 (Consett, Whittonstall) lost its Sunday service; route 3 (Consett, Blanchland, Townfield) lost the diversion via Ramshaw; route 14 (Consett, Shotley Bridge, Edmunbyers, Stanhope) was withdrawn completely. For many years the latter had provided only two journeys a day. Its demise, along with route 2 to Hexham and routes 15 and 77, showed how Venture was unable to obtain the rural route subsidies then becoming available; although assistance was obtained for route 3 and it survived.

Venture was now clearly concentrating on its core profitable activities. In February 1968 Consett local routes 4 (Bridgehill) and 8 (Crookhall) were each increased in frequency from three to four buses per hour. Then in November 1969 route 8 was extended to cover a greater part of Crookhall, which in fact brought it closer to areas served by a competing route of Northern General. A new development in March 1970 was the introduction of express limited stop trips at peak times over route 11 between Consett, the Derwent Valley and Newcastle, numbered as X1.

The best earnings were now from the key routes to Newcastle (5,11,22,24,33, and 44), Consett local routes (4,7,8 and 9), routes 12 and 30 and C & E routes 25 and 31. Progress had also been made with route 17 in west Newcastle. The network was efficiently scheduled using a modern fleet of buses. Reliability was paramount, timetable books were regularly published and newspapers and agents were used to promote the excursions and tours business.

By the late 1960s Venture was operating from depots at Blackhill and High Spen. Its head office remained in Consett but by 1964 had moved to new premises in anticipation of the demolition of 16/17 Princes Street as part of redevelopment in Consett. Depot improvements had taken place from the late 1950s, with a new building replacing two separate ex-Robson Bros properties in High Spen and extensions and improvements at Blackhill to enable the closure of Low Westwood garage, which was originally the home of Venture Bus Services.

Blackhill housed the main workshops for the whole fleet as well as the running depot for Consett area routes. The small depot at Annfield Plain, acquired with the C & E Bus Co Ltd was closed in 1968 and the buses needed for the C & E routes became Blackhill-based. At this stage 48 buses and coaches were allocated at Blackhill and 37 at High Spen.

Varied Activities

Although Venture Transport was primarily an operator of stage carriage bus services, other related activities were also good revenue-earners. For instance, on Stanhope and Blanchland show days there was extensive duplication of services from Consett and Shotley Bridge (for connections from Newcastle) and often fully loaded duplicate buses ran right through from Newcastle via Rowlands Gill and Shotley Bridge to Stanhope or Blanchland - a distance of 25 to 30 miles.

On the excursions front, day trips operated far and wide to places such as Edinburgh, York, Scarborough, Blackpool, the Lake District, the Yorkshire Dales and the Scottish Borders. Excursions to race meetings in the north of England were also very popular. In the summer months, full and half day excursions to the local coastal resorts of Whitley Bay, South Shields and Roker/Seaburn were very popular - on fine days up to 30 vehicles could be employed on such work. It was often a scramble to call out extra drivers as the demand grew towards the early afternoon departures from Consett, Chopwell, Rowlands Gill, High Spen, Greenside and other points. Drivers and vehicles operating morning departures came back for lunchtime departures. The challenge after these had departed was to arrange extra vehicles and drivers for the early evening returns from the coast which were all at the same time. The busiest days were Sundays and school summer holiday weekdays.

A new development in the 1960s was the operation of duplicate vehicles on Saturdays on hire to United for the Newcastle, Whitby, Scarborough, Bridlington services. Some were operated as feeder services from the Consett area through to the Yorkshire resorts and others originated from United's Newcastle Gallowgate bus station. Up to 20 Venture vehicles could be engaged on this activity. When taken together with the company's own private hires and excursions it was a requirement that the whole fleet was available for service. Inevitably supervisory staff waited with "fingers crossed" for the first vehicles to return in the early evening, so that replacement buses were available if needed. The pressure was on, of course, on these busy days but good planning and ingenuity ensured that everything operated as planned.

Football matches provided good revenue. Excursions were operated to all Sunderland home matches at Roker Park. In the case of Newcastle United, the practice was to operate duplicate buses on the various services into Newcastle, as the terminus at Marlborough Crescent bus station was only a short distance from St James Park ground.

The Fleet

Many vehicle types were included in the early fleets of the constituent operators. Details are sketchy but it is likely that after the 1914-18 war ex-War Department lorries, converted for passenger-carrying, were amongst the vehicles used. However, by the mid 1920s Reed Bros was favouring Albions and Venture Bus Services ran mostly Thornycrofts. The Robson Yellow Bus Service had a liking for Dennis buses. Many of the buses were acquired new, but second-hand purchases were also made.

From 1930, both Venture Bus Services and Reed Bros took both new and second-hand buses into stock, in addition to those of acquired firms. There was a selection of Albion, Leyland, Maudslay and

Thornycroft types. However, between 1934 and 1936, apart from one Leyland, all new buses were Maudslays. In total, Venture and Reed Bros had six of the ML3 model and Robson Bros had nine. In 1935/6 there were ten of the advanced SF40 model. These had the engine mounted at the front alongside the driver, with the front axle set back so that the entrance door was opposite the driver forward of the axle. Forty forward-facing seats were achieved, which was a benefit with the area's low bridges preventing the use of double-deckers. These SF40s had Willowbrook bodies. From 1935 through to 1959 that supplier was always chosen for bodywork, apart from two buses bought during the 1939-45 war.

The smaller operators acquired in the 1930s had a wide selection of vehicle types, some of which remained in use with Venture and Reed Bros, but others were soon disposed of. Two impressive ADC 417 buses from J Clydesdale were used for several years, as were two Leyland Lioness machines acquired from Mrs Annie Bessford, one of which was reputed to be the 1928 Motor Show model. The last Maudslay deliveries were three of the ML5 model, delivered in 1936. These had 39-seat Willowbrook bodies, of a style which was to be fitted to all buses bought until the second world war.

In 1937 a change was made back to an earlier supplier when ten Albion Valkyrie SPW141 buses arrived, followed in 1938 by two more and eight of the CX11 model. All had 39-seat bodies. Two similarly bodied Daimler COG5 buses were also acquired in 1938 and seven more were delivered in 1939. Six Willowbrook 32-seat Daimler COG5 luxury coaches also came in 1939.

During the war years the company had to manage with the fleet as it was in 1939, as only two buses could be obtained, in 1942: a new Dennis Lancet with Strachans utility body and a second-hand Daimler CP6 with a Pickering body which had been new to the Lanarkshire Traction Company in 1932; it came to Venture from United Automobile Services.

Venture was optimistic after the war and placed an order for 70 Daimler CVD6 chassis with 35 seat Willowbrook bodywork. In the event only 60 were needed and ten were diverted to Newcastle Corporation Transport. These 60 Daimlers became the typical Venture bus for many years and proved to be highly reliable.

By the mid 1950s it was obvious that larger buses were needed. After trying Sentinel and Atkinson demonstrators Venture took delivery of no fewer than 24 Atkinson Alpha underfloor-engined vehicles between 1955 and 1957. They had Willowbrook bodies; the first 18 were 45-seat buses and the last six had 41 coach seats.

By early 1958 all the prewar vehicles had gone

and a start had been made on the withdrawal of the postwar Daimler CVD6 buses. The Atkinsons proved to be robust and economical machines. However, for 1958 deliveries earlier chassis supplier loyalties prevailed and ten Albion Aberdonian MR11 chassis were ordered, with dual-purpose 41 seat Willowbrook bodies. One 45-seat Aberdonian with a Willowbrook body, which had been built as a demonstrator, also arrived in 1958. Six more 45-seat Aberdonians were delivered in 1959. These particular Willowbrook bodied buses were very light weight, being only 4tons 19cwt unladen. The 17 Aberdonians were very economical vehicles and they managed well in the hilly territory experienced on many of Venture's routes. Two Leyland Tiger Cubs completed the 1959 deliveries. One had a 41 seat Willowbrook Viking coach body and the other carried a 45-seat Willowbrook bus body. Both these had the Albion constant-mesh five-speed gearbox (which the writer enjoyed when on driving duties with the Tiger Cub bus in the 1960s).

At the end of 1959 the first of six Duple bodied Bedford SB coaches was delivered for the 1960 season. This was a new departure for Venture, the idea being to renew the Bedfords on a frequent basis to keep an up to date coach fleet for private hires and the longer distance excursions. Prior to this the dedicated coach fleet had been the 1939 Daimler COG5 vehicles which had been replaced in 1957 by the six 41-seat Atkinsons. The 1960 Bedfords were replaced by six more in 1962 and replacements followed again in 1964 and 1967.

On the service bus front, 1960 saw a return to heavier-weight buses with the delivery of five AEC Reliances with 45-seat Park Royal bodywork. An 11 seat Commer minibus was also bought in 1960, as an experiment in private hire for small parties, but this did not develop and the vehicle was sold in 1963.

Returning to service buses, a further ten 45 seat AEC Reliances arrived in 1961; five were bodied by Weymann and the remainder by Park Royal. For 1962 there was a change of supplier. Venture had hoped to take delivery of eight of the new 36ft-long buses, but delivery could not be arranged that year so ten 30ft-long Leyland Leopards were taken instead. These had bodywork by another new supplier, Alexander of Falkirk. All ten had bus style bodies, but six had 41 coach seats and the other four had 45 seats. The ten 30ft Leyland Leopards were good performers and suited Venture's hilly territory very well.

The change to Alexander as coachwork supplier led to a relationship which was to last until the end of Venture's independent existence. In 1963 the first 36ft-long vehicles arrived. These were five Leyland Leopards with Alexander Y-type bodywork equipped with 51 coach seats. These fine machines set the improved standards of comfort and appearance which Venture required to enhance the quality of its local bus services. They were well received and thereafter all new service buses for the company had this type of body.

However, there was still competition to supply the chassis. AEC supplied six Reliances in 1964 and again in 1965. Thereafter Leyland supplied a further 21 Leopards; six in 1966, three in 1968, six in 1969 and six in 1970. The last six (fleet Nos 285-90) were the final vehicles delivered to Venture as an independent company.

In 1969 serious consideration was given to the possible purchase of Leyland Atlantean or Daimler Fleetline double-deckers; by that time the majority of the low bridges affecting Venture's routes - such a problem to running the services in earlier years - had been removed. This was not to be: dramatic changes were just over the horizon.

Into 1970: the End Approaches

Venture Transport had a highly professional approach to its everyday task of taking people safely and reliably to their destinations. The company was operating over 3 million miles and carrying over 13 million passengers per year. The modern fleet of 84 buses and coaches had an average age of six and a half years. The fleet, in its yellow, maroon and cream livery, looked smart in urban and rural locations.

Nevertheless, the Directors were concerned about the Transport Act 1968, which had created the National Bus Company and the Tyneside Passenger Transport Authority and Executive. It was felt that these new organisations would have a major influence on public transport provision in localities which would be crucial to Venture Transport's future success. No doubt the National Bus Company wished to consolidate its position vis-à-vis the Tyneside PTE and so, on 30th April 1970, Venture Transport was sold to Northern General Transport and was effectively nationalised. It was undoubtedly a case of a willing seller and a willing buyer.

Thus ended nearly sixty years of staunch and efficient independence and on 1st January 1975 Venture Transport ceased operations and its mantle was assumed by Northern General.

Below: V 2337, the Halley charabanc of Reed Bros The chassis was commandeered by the military for the 1914-18 war and the business effectively ceased in this period. (GEH Collection)

>> Opposite page: A selection of early tickets, including a Venture Bus Services quarterly pass; Bessford's special 12-journey cheap ticket for Rowlands Gill to Newcastle; a Venture Transport 12-journey ticket; Venture and Reed Bros Bell Punch tickets ranging from ½d to 2/6d; Venture Transport and C & E Bus Company Bellgraphics. (GEH Collection)

Issued by Venture Bus Services, Ltd., Ebchester. Tel 22. 1584

QUARTERLY PASS

Name ....Pass No ....

From ....to ....

Issued ....expires ....

To be shown on demand.
N.B. By mutual arrangement this pass is available on
Buses of Venture Bus Services, Ltd., and Reed Bros. Ltd
NOT TRANSFERABLE.

BESSFORD'S 1770

Special Cheap Ticket

Name ....

1	ROWLANDS GILL	7
2		8
3	BESSFORD'S **Special**	9
4	NEWCASTLE	10
5	**5/-**	11
6	Not Transferable.	12

Pc 4857

VENTURE & REED BROS.
RETURN
4D

Venture & Reed Bros.

Issued subject to conditions
shown in Company's Notices
in Time-tables and Buses.

IN	SINGLE	OUT
	4d	

Bell Punch Company, London. B6904

Pc 4857

Bb 6704

VENTURE & REED BROS.

1		9
2		10
3		11
4	**1**D	12
5		13
6	**2**	14
7		15
8		16

THIS TICKET MUST BE
SHOWN ON DEMAND.
Bell Punch Co., Uxbridge A3450

N 6248 N 6248

VENTURE   VENTURE
TRANSPORT   TRANSPORT
CO. N/C. LTD.   CO. N/C. LTD.

JNY	COND. INIT.	A	B	COND. INIT.	JNY
12					2
11					3
10		Holder's Signature			4
9					5
M	12 JOURNEY TICKET				6
F					7
X					8

NOT VALID UNLESS PRICE PRINTED

A 5317

VENTURE & REED BROS.

IN	ISSUED SUBJECT TO COMPANY'S REGULATIONS.	OUT
EXCURSION	TWO SHILLINGS **2/6** SIXPENCE	TICKET

THIS TICKET MUST BE
SHOWN ON DEMAND.
Bell Punch Company, London. C4971

Ca 8308

VENTURE & REED BROS.
RETURN
11D

Venture & Reed Bros.

Issued subject to conditions
shown in Company's Notices
in Time-tables and Buses.

IN	SINGLE	OUT
	11d	

Bell Punch Company, London. B6903

Ca 8308

VENTURE TRANSPORT Co. (Newcastle) LTD.

SHILLINGS	PENCE	Stage From
SINGLE		
RETURN		

Issued subject to the Company's Regulations   Stage To

22343 R0

Bell Punch Company, Limited, London.

C. & E. BUS CO. LTD.
& ASSOCIATED COMPANIES

SHILLINGS	PENCE	Stage From
SINGLE		
RETURN		

Issued subject to the Company's Regulations   Stage To

Ea 07760

Bell Punch Company, Limited, London.

Upper: One of two Albion buses delivered to Reed Bros in 1918, photographed at Sunniside. These enabled their bus business to restart after the war.

Centre: Reed Bros Dennis bus (**CN 1091**) new in 1922. This picture was taken at Chopwell and the bus would be operating the route between Chopwell, Hamsterley Colliery, Rowlands Gill and Newcastle started by Reed Bros after the war.

Lower: **PT 8532** was a 1926 Thornycroft of Venture Bus Services. It is seen at Newcastle. The rear view shows the City of Newcastle licence plate and the 20 seats hackney carriage plate. *(All: GEH Collection)*

Above: The horse-drawn "Venture" coach is pictured here with Messrs Harrison and Richardson and one of their buses which used the Venture fleetname.

Below: Venture Bus Services Thornycroft No. **7** (**PT 9537**) was new in 1927. This 20-seat bus was used on the Consett, Newcastle route. *(Both: GEH Collection)*

Above: A Reed Bros Albion bus, showing Venture fleet names. This was one of several similar buses acquired in the late 1920s. The drawing shown inside the rear cover of this book is of one of these vehicles.

Below: Another Reed Bros Albion, again showing Venture fleetnames, is pictured at the then recently purchased Blackhill depot, probably in 1930. *(Both: GEH Collection)*

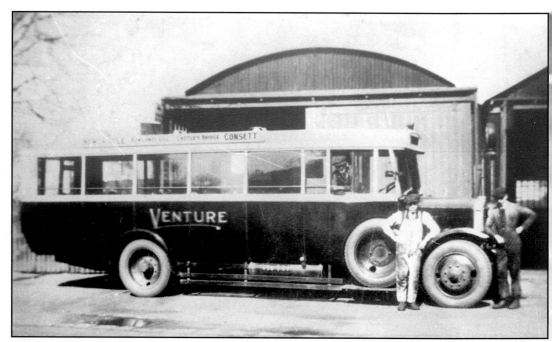

Above: J R. & R B Parker of Chopwell operated this 1924 SPA. The **S**ocietà Ligure **P**iemontese **A**utomobili was an Italian chassis manufacturer which came under the control of Fiat after 1925. Parker's fleet number **4** was registered **PT 2476** and the 14-seat body was built by H Young of Chester-le-Street. The bus was used on Parker's routes between Chopwell and Newcastle via Rowlands Gill.

Below: In 1928 Parker acquired Thornycroft No. **5** (**PT 2088**). It had a 20-seat body also built by H Young. *(Both: GEH Collection)*

Above: J Clydesdale of Chopwell operated on the same routes as Parker between Chopwell and Newcastle. This De Dion (PT 7491) was new in 1926 and is pictured at the Marlborough Crescent terminus in Newcastle. The Leyland PLSC Lion (**PT 8580**) to the left of the picture was operated by Atkinson & Browell of Consett (ABC) on their Newcastle, Sunniside, Dipton, Consett route.

Below: Clydesdale operated two ADC 417 buses, the first of which, **TN 6398** was new in 1927. This 26-seat bus is seen here at Marlborough Crescent. *(Both: GEH Collection)*

Above: The second ADC for Clydesdale's Bus Service (**TN 7848**) was new in 1928. This view of it is another taken at Marlborough Crescent.

Below: The last bus purchased by Clydesdale was this 28-seat Albion (**UP 2860**), which was new in 1929. The proprietor is standing on the vehicle's step in this view, again taken at Marlborough Crescent. *(Both: GEH Collection)*

Above: Mrs Annie Bessford operated between High Spen, Rowlands Gill and Newcastle. This Leyland Lioness (**UP 147**) had 28 seats and was new in 1927. It was photographed awaiting its departure time for High Spen at Marlborough Crescent. This bus is reputed to have been a 1928 Motor Show model on the Leyland Motors stand.

Below: John Elphinstone Walker, of Heatherlea Garage, Edmundbyers operated "The Pioneer Bus Service" between Blanchland, Edmundbyers, Shotley Bridge and Consett until he sold the business to Reed Bros in 1930. This small bus is a Reo (**PT 2698**) new in 1924. It is pictured at Blanchland outside The Lord Crewe Arms. *(Both: GEH Collection)*

Above: The Yellow Bus Service was operated by Robson Bros and had branches based at High Spen and Consett. This 1926 Dennis (**PT 7022**) was photographed in Bewick Street, Newcastle awaiting its departure for High Spen via Blaydon and Greenside.

Below: Robson Bros had their Consett depot at a place called No. One on the outskirts of the town. This picture, probably taken in 1930, shows the proprietors with a line-up of Gilford and Dennis buses in a street opposite the depot. *(Both: GEH Collection)*

<< *Opposite page:* Following the acquisition of Robson's Yellow Bus Service, the Venture and Reed Bros subsidiary - Robson Bros Ltd - acquired in 1935 three of the advanced Maudslay SF40 model. Willowbrook 40-seat bodies were fitted to these buses as shown here on No. **68** (**APT 587**).

Above: A 1932 acquisition by Reed Bros was this 32-seat Leyland-bodied Leyland LT5 No. **25** (**UP 6922**). This picture was taken when the bus was new, outside the Plaza cinema buildings at Consett, whence buses departed for Newcastle in the days before Consett bus station was built.

Below: Reed Bros bought a new Leyland LT5A in 1934, fitted with a 32-seat rear-entrance Burlingham coach body. It had fleet number **29** and was registered **UP 9170**. Whereas No. 25 above was in Reed's green livery, No. 29 had the yellow and maroon livery by then in use by Venture & Reed Bros. *(All: GEH collection)*

Above: In 1935 and 1936 Venture & Reed Bros and their Robson Bros subsidiary took delivery of a total of ten 40-seat Willowbrook-bodied Maudslay SF40 buses. Reed had four, Robsons and Venture had three each. Reed Bros No. **31** (**APT 142**) is shown here in the yellow and maroon livery. The three Robson vehicles retained the Yellow Bus Service livery until the formation of Venture Transport in 1938.

Below: Three Willowbrook-bodied Maudslay ML5 buses arrived in 1936: one for Reeds and two for Venture. This is Reed Bros No. **37** (**AUP 334**) at Blackhill depot when new.

>> *Opposite page:* Ten Albion Valkyrie SPW141 buses were purchased in 1937 followed by two more in 1938 along with eight of the Valkyrie CX11 type. All had Willowbrook 39-seat bodies. Reed Bros No. **43** (**BUP 553**) is pictured here when new in 1937. *(All: GEH collection)*

Upper: Albion Valkyrie fleet No. **41** (**BUP 552**) in 1947 snow. *(GEH Collection)*

Centre: Albion CX11 No. **82** (**CUP 888**) is seen at Marlborough Crescent bus station, Newcastle awaiting departure for High Spen via Rowlands Gill. *(A D Mennear)*

Lower: Albion fleet No. **86** (**DPT 337**) at Marlborough Crescent in 1951 operating the former Robson Bros route to Greenside via Folly. Albion No. **84** stands behind for route 22 to Chopwell via Ryton. Alongside is United's Eastern Coach Works-rebodied Leyland Tiger TS8 **BHN 272** waiting to leave for Ryton Village via Scotswood and Blaydon on United's service 1A. *(Alan Cross)*

Upper: Albion Valkyrie CX11 No. **87** (**DPT 338**) at Marlborough Crescent soon after the end of the second world war, still showing white markings on the front mudguards. It was operating to High Spen via Ryton. *(R C Davis)*

Centre: This Albion, which was fleet number **88** and registered **DPT 339**, is seen at Ryton in the early 1950s en route for High Spen. *(GEH Collection)*

Lower: Six Daimler COG5 coaches with bodies seating 32 by Willowbrook were delivered in 1939. This mid 1950s picture shows No. **95** (**DUP 210**) at the Bridgehill, Bagnall's Farm terminus, replacing failed Daimler CVD6 No. **119** (**GPT 52**). *(GEH)*

Above: The Willowbrook body fitted to Daimler COG5 No. **97** (**DUP 607**) was of a different style to those of the other Daimler buses delivered at around the same time in that there was no route number indicator. In this early post war view at Consett, it had just arrived from Newcastle on service 5 via Leadgate. *(GEH collection)*

Below: The more typical body type fitted to the prewar Daimlers is shown on No. **99** (**EPT 246**) at Consett bus station in the early postwar years. Behind is one of the Daimler coaches and also a Bedford of C R Robson which had arrived on his route from Hexham via Slaley. *(R C Davis)*

Above: Private Hires were always important business for Venture. This view at the end of the 1940s shows a convoy led by Daimler No. **99**, followed by an Albion Valkyrie, Daimler No. **97** and a postwar Daimler CVD6. The location was Pontop between Consett and Annfield Plain. The likely destination would be the coast at Seaburn, near Sunderland.

Below: Venture received only one new bus during the second world war. A Dennis Lancet with Strachan 35-seat bodywork, No. **104** (**EUP 910**) was delivered in 1942. *(Both: GEH Collection).*

<< *Opposite page:* Great confidence in the future led to the delivery of sixty Daimler CVD6 buses with 35-seat Willowbrook bodywork in the years 1946 to 1948. The fleet numbers were 106 to 165 and this is No. **106** (**FUP 388**) when new. The traditional "rising sun" fleetname in use at the time was a well known feature of Venture buses. *(GEH Collection)*

Above: Daimler No. **109** (**FUP 391**) at Consett bus station when new. It is on the departure stand for route 2 to Whittonstall. In the background can be seen Venture's head office at 16/17, Princes Street, and also an AEC single-decker of Northern General Transport. *(R C Davis)*

Below: Daimler No. **117** (**FUP399**) at Blackhill depot displaying a poster for O.P.P.A. (Omnibus Passengers Protection Association). This body sought to influence public opinion so as to oppose the postwar Labour Government's proposals to extend the nationalisation of the bus industry in the North-East. *(GEH Collection)*

Above: Daimler No. **114** (**FUP 396**) at Consett bus station in the early 1960s. Behind is Northern General Transport No. **1817** (**HCN 117**), a Burlingham-bodied AEC Reliance. This had arrived in Consett from Waskerley on route 17, which was probably Northern's most rural service, operating on Saturdays only and then soon to be withdrawn. *(GEH)*

Below: Daimler (fleet number **145**, **GPT 973**) in flood conditions at Snows Green near Shotley Bridge. *(G Coxon)*

Above: From 1959 the yellow and maroon livery was modified to include a cream roof, with maroon confined to the body waistrail and wheels (and mudguards on the remaining Daimlers), epitomised by Daimler No. **121** (**GPT 54**) at Blackhill depot in 1962. This 1946 bus was finally withdrawn from service in 1963.

Below: An interesting night photograph of two Daimlers (Nos **123** and **163**) in Blackhill depot in 1962. These buses were withdrawn in 1963 and 1964 respectively. *(Both: G Coxon)*

Above: On 9th February 1963 the Consett to Blanchland service was restarted after a lengthy suspension caused by heavy snow in the North Pennines. The first bus through was Daimler No. **161** (**JPT 549**) photographed on arrival at Blanchland.

Below: An impression of the conditions on that February day can be gained from this picture of the Daimler near Carterway Heads on the return trip to Consett. *(Both: GEH)*

Upper: The last ten Daimlers delivered in 1948 were to a higher body specification with more luxurious seats and enhanced interior and exterior trim. Fleet number 160 (**JPT 548**) was photographed when new. *(GEH Collection)*

Centre: For its last few years in service, until withdrawal in 1964, Daimler No. 163 was fitted with seats from earlier withdrawn examples, given the revised livery and a door and cab conversion to make it suitable for driver only operation. *(GEH)*

Lower: One of the Daimlers outlived all others with the Company. Number 113 (**FUP 395**) was converted to a towing wagon after withdrawal in 1959 and was kept for this purpose until 1969. This picture shows it by the fuelling bay at Blackhill depot. *(GEH)*

<< *Opposite page:* After the large intake of Daimlers between 1946 and 1948 no more new vehicles arrived until 1955, when twelve Atkinson buses were delivered in two separate batches. This illustration shows Nos. **167-9** (**RPT 127-9**) when new. These were the Atkinson Alpha BPL745H model, fitted with handsome 45-seat bodies by Willowbrook. As can be seen, the fleetname style was also revised at this time. *(GEH Collection)*

Above: Fleet No. **175** (**RUP 436**) was from the second batch of Atkinsons; it is seen here in the late 1950s at Consett. *(GEH)*

Below: A third batch of Atkinson Alpha BPL745H buses was placed into service in 1956, again with Willowbrook 45-seat bodies but which had a modified front panel profile. Fleet No. **181** (**TPT 111**) was at Consett bus station in the early 1960s and shows the application of the cream painted roof in place of maroon. *(GEH)*

Above: Atkinson No. **180** (**TPT 110**) approaching Consett on the steep climb from Blackhill in the mid 1960s. Such conditions were common in the winter months. *(G Coxon)*

Below: An interesting comparison at Consett in 1960 showing, from left to right, 1956 Atkinson No. **182**, 1958 Albion No. **199** and 1957 Atkinson No. **189**. The three different liveries will be explained in the following pages. *(GEH Collection)*

>> *Opposite page:* The final six Atkinson Alphas were delivered in 1957 with Willowbrook bodies fitted with 41 coach seats and painted in a cream and maroon livery. The first two, Nos **184/5** (**VPT 547/8**) show how attractive these vehicles were. They were initially used to replace the 1939 Daimler coaches, which at various times had also been painted mainly cream with maroon trim. These Alphas were fast too, with their constant-mesh David Brown "overdrive" gearboxes, but their five cylinder Gardner diesel engines slowed them down in hilly terrain. *(GEH Collection)*

39

Above: The cream Atkinsons soon appeared on service and No. **189** (**VPT 552**) is seen in 1958 at Consett between trips on route 11 to Newcastle. *(GEH)*

Below: Following delivery of six Bedford coaches in 1959/60, the cream Atkinsons were regarded as normal service buses and were soon painted yellow, maroon and cream as shown on No. **187** (**VPT 550**) at Consett. Initially the coach seats were retained, but later they were replaced with 45 refurbished bus seats from withdrawn Daimlers. *(GEH Collection)*

Upper: The C & E Bus Co Ltd subsidiary operated a frequent local service from Stanley to Dipton and Flint Hill via Annfield Plain and after this 1951 acquisition Venture buses were always used "On hire to C & E". Daimlers were used for many years and No. **165** is seen here on the parking area behind Stanley Front Street. *(G. Coxon)*

Centre: After the withdrawal of the Daimlers the usual C & E allocation was the six Atkinsons, Nos. 184-9. The C & E routes 25 and 31 operated from Stanley Front Street where No. **184 (VPT 547)** is pictured awaiting departure for Dipton via Flint Hill. Venture had introduced a further new fleetname style by the time of this 1966 picture. *(GEH)*

Lower: By late 1968 the C & E routes had been converted to driver-only operation and AEC Reliances had replaced the Atkinsons, by then withdrawn. Also, the small garage at New Kyo, near Stanley, had been closed and the fleet was transferred to Blackhill. This 1969 view shows Park Royal-bodied AEC Reliance No. **227 (1890 PT)** at Stanley Front Street, soon to depart for Flint Hill via Dipton. *(GEH)*

<< *Opposite page:* In 1958/9 Venture acquired 17 Albion Aberdonian MRII buses fitted with Willowbrook bodies. The first ten, Nos. 190-9 (XUP 392-401), had 41 high-backed seats and were the first new vehicles delivered in yellow and maroon with cream roofs. They also had an unpainted aluminium area below the waist rail, although this soon looked rather drab and in later years was painted yellow. Fleet No. **196** (**XUP 398**) was new in this illustration. *(GEH Collection)*

Above: This April 1965 picture of Albion No. **193** (**XUP 395**) shows the later fleetname style as used on vehicles where the fleetname would not fit the waist rail, although in this case the vehicle has a small fleetname in the latter position. It was photographed at Blackhill depot after a repaint. *(GEH)*

Below: At the end of 1958 a further Willowbrook-bodied Albion was delivered. It was an unregistered demonstrator which became No. **200** (**164 BUP**). This 45-seater was pictured in Consett bus station when it first entered service in January 1959. The buses behind are Northern General Transport Metro-Cammell-bodied Guy Arab No. **1635** (**CU 7635**) of 1955; a Northern 1954 AEC Monocoach and a Venture Daimler. *(GEH)*

Above: By 1964 Albion No. **200** had been fitted for driver-only operation and some additional embellishment had been fitted to the front panel. The bus was awaiting its next trip on Consett local route 6 to Templetown, which was scheduled to take four minutes. This small suburb of Consett was almost surrounded by the large Consett steel works. Indeed on some trips this service diverted via the Hounsgill part of the steel plant at shift-change times to pick up or set down employees. The Northern bus behind is No. **1728** (**FCN 728**) a Weymann bodied AEC Reliance. *(GEH)*

Below: Albion No. **200** again, at rest at Blackhill depot in the mid 1960s in company with Atkinson Alpha No. **187**. *(G Coxon)*

Above: The six Albion Aberdonians delivered in 1959 had 45-seat Willowbrook bodies. Their unladen weight at 4tons 19cwts allowed good fuel economy along with a decent performance in Venture's hilly operating area. This is No. **202** (**166 BUP**) when new. *(GEH Collection)*

Below: Albion No. **201** (**165 BUP**) at Consett bus station in 1959 awaiting departure on Consett local route 7 to the Hat & Feather Inn via Leadgate and Bradley. Venture operated on this route every 30 minutes, as did Armstrongs Motor Services of Ebchester, thus providing a joint 15-minute frequency. There was a difference however: Venture vehicles only also operated via Pont Head Estate in Leadgate. *(GEH)*

Upper: High Spen depot operated two town services in Prudhoe, with buses that had travelled from Chopwell to Prudhoe on the rural route via Hedley on the Hill and Mickley. All three routes were numbered as 15. Venture ceased operating these routes after 27th April 1968 as part of a service coordination scheme with United Automobile Services. Albion No. **202** was in Prudhoe Front Street on 13th April 1968. *(GEH)*

Centre: Also on 13th April 1968, Albion No. **202** is seen passing down Neale Street, Prudhoe towards West Wylam Estate. *(GEH)*

Lower: The town services in Prudhoe used roads with steep inclines. This 13th April 1968 view shows Albion No. **202** en route to Drawback Close. *(GEH)*

Above: Two Leyland Tiger Cubs were also purchased in 1959. Fleet No. **207** (**550 CPT**) was fitted with a Willowbrook Viking 41-seat coach body and is believed to have originally been an unregistered demonstrator. It was pictured when new in Victoria Road Consett, awaiting a private hire party. *(GEH Collection)*

Below: The Tiger Cub coach was rarely seen on local routes, but this late 1960s picture shows it at Consett bus station operating the Consett feeder service for the Yorkshire Coast Express to Butlin's Holiday Camp, Filey, on hire to United Automobile Services. *(GEH)*

Above: The second 1959 Leyland Tiger Cub had the last Willowbrook body supplied to Venture and was fitted out as a 45-seat service bus. In this 1963 view at Consett, No. **208 (601 EPT)** was showing some body damage suffered in the ice and snow of 1963's difficult winter conditions.

Below: Tiger Cub No. **208** was used to operate the first trip from High Westwood and Medomsley to Consett on 22nd January 1963 after heavy snow falls. It is shown here leaving Medomsley on Fines Road, for Consett via No. One. *(Both: GEH)*

Upper: The author drove the Tiger Cub No. **208** on the last day of operation of route 2 between Consett and Hexham on 4th March 1967. It is seen here at Consett prior to operating the 1.00pm trip to Hexham. It is alongside a Northern General Transport AEC Monocoach with Park Royal body (No. **1611, DCN 911**). *(GEH)*

Centre: A rare picture of a Venture bus in Hexham bus station. Venture No. **208** on 4th March 1967, ready to operate the 2.00pm trip back to Consett. It is alongside United Automobile Services Bristol MW No. **U693 (8693 HN)**, which was operating the 1.10pm journey from Allendale via Hexham to Newcastle on route 37. *(GEH)*

Lower: The author also drove the last ever trips on route 14 between Consett and Stanhope in September 1968. This very rural route, over wild moorland in the North Pennines, had provided only two return trips a day for many years. Tiger Cub No. **208** was photographed at Consett bus station about to depart on the 7.30pm run to Stanhope.

(T F Hutchinson)

<< Opposite page: There was a complete change of manufacturers for the 1960 delivery of five buses: AEC Reliances with 45-seat Park Royal bodywork. This picture shows them leaving the factory in convoy led by No. **218** (**783 HUP**). *(GEH Collection)*

Upper: Three Park Royal bodied AEC Reliances unloading at Victoria Road, Consett in 1962. The leading bus, No. **218**, has arrived from Blanchland. *(GEH)*

Centre: In this 1966 picture of Park Royal-bodied Reliance No. **215** some work on the front panel and a fresh repaint had improved the appearance. The large front fleetname was not continued with, but it did look attractive. The bus was at Consett bus station waiting to depart on Consett local route 9 to Shotley Bridge Hospital. *(GEH)*

Lower: The sole minibus was a Commer VH1500 11-seater bought in 1960. Number **220** (**744 PT**) was by the fuel pumps at Blackhill depot. *(G Coxon)*

<< *Opposite page:* For 1961 ten more 45-seat AEC Reliances were purchased; the body order for them was split equally between Weymann (Nos. 221-5, 1884-8PT) and Park Royal (Nos. 226-30, 1889-93 PT). This is Weymann-bodied No. **222** when new. *(GEH Collection)*

Above: As part of a coordination scheme with United Automobile Services, which was implemented on Sunday 28th April 1968, major changes were made to Venture and United routes along the south side of the Tyne Valley from Newcastle via Blaydon and Ryton. On the first day of new Venture route 24, Weymann-bodied AEC Reliance No. **223** operated the first trip at 10.54am from Greenside, Rockwood Hill. It is pictured at the Folly near Greenside. *(GEH)*

Below: The Weymann-bodied Reliances spent most of their time at High Spen depot, but in this 1962 view No. **225** was in use on Consett local route 8. *(R C Davis)*

Above: Another complete change of chassis and body suppliers occurred in 1962 with the delivery of ten Alexander-bodied Leyland Leopards, Nos. 231-40 (9531-40 PT). The first six had 41 high-backed seats and the others had 45 bus seats. This 1963 picture shows No. **238** at Blackhill depot. *(G Coxon)*

Below: Leyland Leopard No. **237** had received front panel modifications by the time of this picture taken at Consett bus station on 27th September 1969. The bus was operating on Consett local route 4 to Bridgehill, which operated every fifteen minutes, taking nine minutes for the mainly downhill outward trip and ten minutes for the more onerous return journey. *(GEH)*

Above: From the mid 1960s Venture became very involved in working on hire to United Automobile Services on summer Saturdays on the Yorkshire Coast Express services from Tyneside to Whitby, Scarborough, Filey and Bridlington. The arrangement suited both parties - United could secure many vehicles from one operator and Venture could employ vehicles which were available on Saturdays between their Monday to Friday work and summer Sunday excursions. Leyland Leopard No. **233** is pictured here reversing off the departure platform at United's Newcastle Gallowgate depot.

Below: Four Venture Alexander Y-type-bodied vehicles await their turn for loading at Gallowgate: three AEC Reliances (Nos. **267**, **259** and **258**) and Leyland Leopard No. **249**. The seating capacity of these 51 seaters was particularly suitable for United's needs on this operation. *(Both: GEH)*

<< Opposite page: Venture was impressed by the Alexander Y-type body for its bus fleet replacements from 1963 onwards. These attractive vehicles raised standards for passenges on local routes, and their better-quality seating meant that they could be used on the local and medium distance private hires and excursions which were important business for Venture. Thirty-eight Y-type-bodied vehicles were bought between 1963 and 1970, all with 51 seats. Twelve were on AEC Reliance chassis and 26 were Leyland Leopards. The first five were manual gearbox Leopard PSU3/3R models of which No. **249** (**6249 UP**) is shown here when new in 1963. *(GEH Collection)*
Above: The first two Y-type-bodied Leopards (Nos. 247/8) were delivered with the then standard fleet name style. This was changed to a more modern standard from No. 249 onwards, as shown on the previous page. This illustration shows No. **247** ready for its first duty in 1963 - an excursion to the local coast. Behind is an Albion on similar duties and an Atkinson Alpha. The picture was taken on a sunny Sunday at Consett. *(GEH)*
Below: Leopard No. **248** is crossing the old Scotswood "chain bridge" in this 1963 view. This bridge was used by all Venture routes into Newcastle and because of a weight restriction these new, larger buses could cross with no more than 38 passengers on board. Initially this problem was overcome by using a diversion via the High Level Bridge for fully loaded peak-hour duplicates and the bus being duplicated was scheduled with a smaller vehicle for its normal route via Scotswood Bridge. Fortunately a new bridge was being built and eventually the problem was overcome. *(GEH Collection)*

Above: In summer 1968, Leyland No. **247** (**6247 UP**) awaits time for its departure from Consett to Butlin's Filey Camp on hire to United. Next to it Northern's fourteen-year-old AEC Monocoach, No. **1608** (**DCN 908**), is ready for its next trip. *(GEH)*

Below: The first six Alexander bodies on AEC Reliance chassis for Venture were delivered in 1964 (Nos. 258-63, CPT 258-63B). In this picture taken at Stanhope Market Place on 16th May 1965 No. **261** was operating a tour of Venture depots and routes for the Northern Branch of the Omnibus Society. The point at the rear of the bus was the terminus for Venture route 14 (Shotley Bridge, Edmundbyers, Stanhope). *(G Coxon)*

Above: The second batch of six Alexander-bodied Reliances arrived in 1965 (Nos. 264-9, HPT 264-9C). In this Sunday view at Consett in July 1965 No. **267** awaits its trip to Newcastle on route 11. The panel below the windscreen showing VTC had a folding flap which could indicate that the bus was driver-only operated. This feature was not repeated on subsequent deliveries. The bus behind is one of Northern's Weymann-bodied AEC Reliances delivered in 1956.

Below: Six Leyland Leopards, Nos. 270-5 (RUP 270-5D), were new for 1966. Number **272** is seen here at Consett bus station in 1966 on route 4 to Bridgehill. Leopard No. **240** is leaving for Blanchland on route 3. A Morris Oxford taxi stands outside the Princes Street office which was soon to be vacated and demolished. *(Both: GEH)*

Above: The next Alexander Y-type-bodied vehicles were three Leylands in 1978 (Nos. 276-8, YUP 576-8F). These had more luxurious seats than were fitted in either the earlier or subsequent batches. On 2nd April 1968 No. **276** leaves Consett for Newcastle on route 11. The building works behind the bus were for Venture's new head office at 37, Medomsley Road, Consett. *(GEH)*

Below: AEC Reliance No. **258** suffered fire damage in late 1968 and was returned to the Alexander factory at Falkirk for repairs. On 18th February 1969 it was photographed at Falkirk next to two new Leyland Atlanteans for Newcastle Corporation Transport. Snow was starting to fall, but the Reliance was driven back to Blackhill that day via Edinburgh, then using the A68 road through Jedburgh, Carter Bar, Otterburn and Corbridge. *(GEH)*

Upper: Venture's 1969 intake of new buses was a further six Leyland Leopards (Nos. 279-84, EPT 79-84G) and No. **281** is seen in this picture at Alexander's factory ready to leave for the journey south to Venture's Blackhill depot.

Centre: The last new buses for Venture as a private company were six more of the popular Alexander-bodied Leyland Leopards (Nos. 285-90, HUP 385-90H). These were collected from Alexander's Falkirk factory in March 1970. This view shows three of the buses shortly before they left for Blackhill. It will be noticed that these final six vehicles did not have the traditional Leyland Leopard badge, which had been replaced by a plainer device.

Lower: On Sunday 26th April 1970, the Northern Branch of the Omnibus Society made a final visit to Venture. For the last part of the tour the party travelled on the first Alexander Y-type-bodied Leyland, No. **247**, which had just been recertified and painted. This picture was taken that afternoon at the Townfield terminus of the Blanchland to Consett route. By a happy coincidence the service car (to use Venture parlance) on the Blanchland route that day was the virtually new Y type, No. **289**. This produced a unique picture just four days before Venture ceased to be a private company. *(All: GEH)*

Upper: The policy of buying batches of six Bedford coaches with Duple bodies, and renewing them after two or three years, commenced in 1959. The first of the initial six was No. **209** (**602 EPT**), delivered in 1959 and the others arrived for the 1960 season as Nos. 210-4 (603-7 EPT). The Bedford coaches were not intended for bus service work at Venture, although many vehicles bought primarily for bus work had seating which made them suitable for local private hires and excursions. However, on very rare occasions, a Bedford would be used on service, but only in an emergency to avoid lost mileage - which was never tolerated at Venture. The initial six Bedfords were replaced in 1962 by six similar coaches, Nos. 241-6 (9541-6 PT). *(GEH Collection)*

Centre: Six more replacement Bedfords arrived in 1964 as Nos. 252-7 (APT 752-7B). Number **257** is shown at Consett on private hire duties. *(GEH).*

Lower: The last six Bedfords were delivered in 1967 and were given fleet numbers in a new sequence as **VC1-6** (**SUP 201-6E**). This line up at Blackhill was photographed on 3rd April 1967 when they were new. *(GEH)*

Above: Many demonstrators were tried over the years. One of the most significant was this Burlingham-bodied Atkinson, seen here on excursion duties. This led to an order for 24 chassis of this type as the company's first underfloor engined buses. *(R C Davis)*

Lower: In October 1966 a Daimler Roadliner (**CVC 124C**) was tried at Consett and used on a variety of services, but an order did not result. *(GEH)*

Above: This rear-engined Albion Viking demonstrator (**EGG 559C**), with Alexander body, was also tried in 1966 and is seen here about to depart Consett for Newcastle. Although the company had a long association with Albion, no order was placed. The Plaxton-bodied Leyland Tiger Cub on the left of this picture at Consett bus station belonged to Armstrongs Motor Services, of Majestic Garage, Ebchester. Armstrongs had been pioneer motor coach operators between Newcastle and London via the Great North Road, trading as Majestic Saloon Coaches. However, they sold that business to United in 1932. The Leyland Tiger Cub was operating on the Consett to Hat & Feather Inn route, which Armstrongs served on a coordinated basis with Venture route 7. Their involvement in the Hat & Feather route came with the business of James Cowling of Consett, who had operated on the route for many years alongside Venture's predecessor, Robson Bros.

Below: AEC Swift **LYY 827D** was also demonstrated in 1966 and this view shows it at Consett bus station waiting to leave for Newcastle. No order was placed. By this stage Venture had decided to continue buying Alexander-bodied Leyland Leopards. These had proved most suitable and reliable for the company's diverse requirements, particularly on its network of bus routes. *(Both: GEH)*